MW01615230

Published by Daoudi Publishing LLC
ISBN: 978-1-960809-23-0

Husband I Keep Searching for Answers...

A Companion Grief Journal for Widows,
with an Open Letter for Healing
After the Loss of a Husband
(Remembrance Journal for Wives)

Evelyn Harrington

I Keep Searching for Answers Journals

TABLE OF CONTENTS

INTRODUCTION

By Evelyn Harrington

Grief is not just about loss, it's about learning to live with love that has nowhere to go. if you are holding this journal, know that whatever you're feeling is valid. the pain, the questions, the memories, and even the silence, all of it deserves space.

Losing a husband changes everything. you may find yourself searching for answers, replaying moments, or wishing for words left unspoken. you may feel overwhelmed or unsure of what to feel at all. that's okay. grief isn't a straight path, and healing isn't about forgetting, it's about making room for what you carry inside.

This journal is here to support you, offering a safe space to express, reflect, and process at your own pace. the prompts inside will help you navigate loss, honor your emotions, and remind you that you are not alone.

Write when you're ready. be honest with yourself. your story, your grief, and your love for your husband will always matter.

With warmth and understanding,
Evelyn Harrington

HOW TO USE THIS JOURNAL

There is no right or wrong way to use this journal. Some prompts may feel natural to answer, while others may be difficult. That's okay. If a prompt feels too heavy, you can:

- Write without stopping for one minute. don't worry about grammar, structure, or making sense. just let your thoughts pour onto the page, unfiltered.

- Pause and take a deep breath. give yourself permission to feel without judgment.

- Write from someone else's perspective. imagine what your loved one might say to you, or how a friend would respond to your emotions.

- Read the prompt out loud. saying the words first can help you process them before writing anything down.

IF YOU EVER FEEL STUCK, START WITH:

- Write down what you can answer today. if a prompt feels too big, break it down. answer just a small piece, and leave the rest for another time. some prompts may feel easier with time.

This journal is here for you, without expectations or timelines. Use it at your own pace, in whatever way helps you process your loss. Every word, every pause, and every tear matters.

This Journal Belongs To:

_____

MY FAMILY TREE

"Family is like a tree, its roots keep us grounded, and
its branches help us grow."

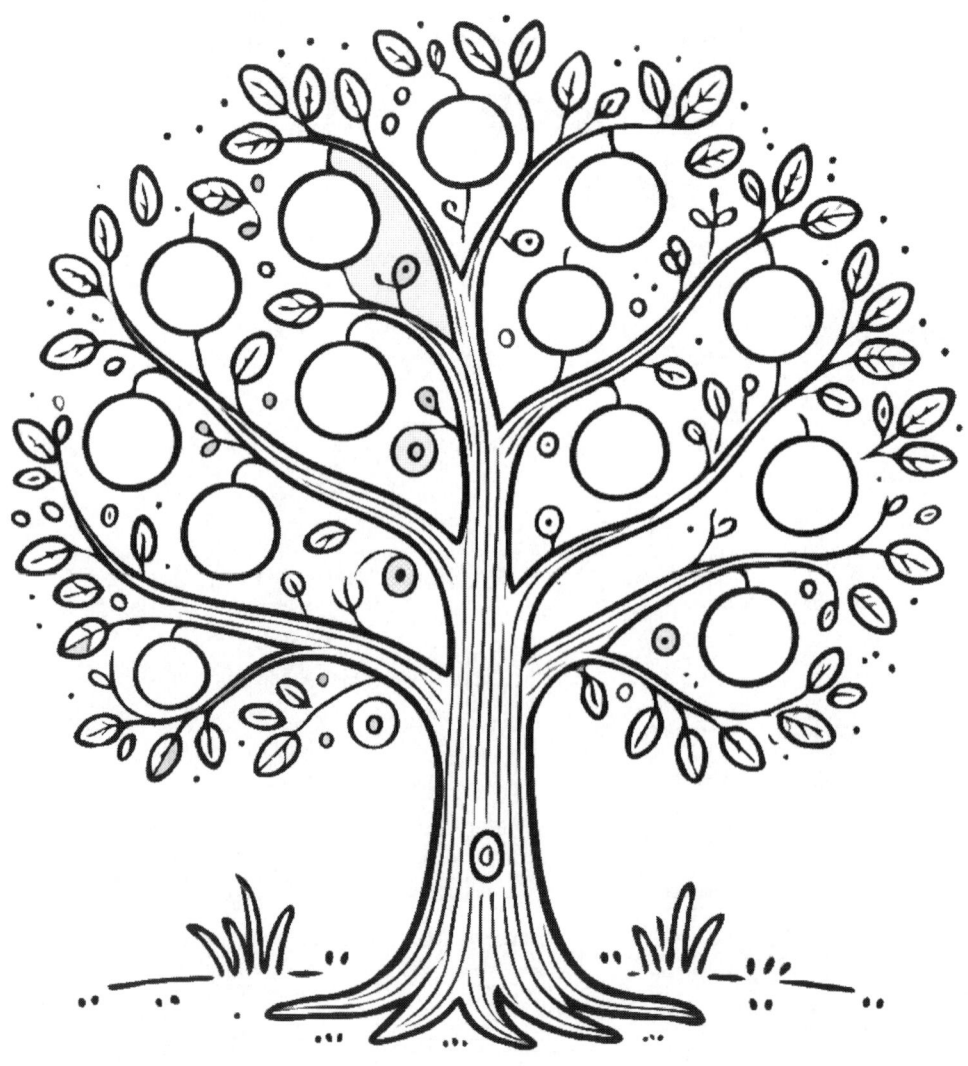

A LOOK AT MY HUSBAND'S LIFE

"A husband's love doesn't end with goodbye, it lives on in
every moment, memory, and quiet strength he left behind."
— Unknown

My husband's full name: _____

His birth date: _____

Date of death:_____

Where my husband was born:_____

The job he was most proud of: _____

His favorite food: _____

A phrase or saying he always used: _____

His favorite song or artist: _____

A hobby he loved the most: _____

A place he always wanted to visit: _____

Things he loved the most: _____

Things he absolutely couldn't stand: _____

His best quality that i admire: _____

One habit of his that always made me laugh: _____

Our favorite thing to do together:_____

His biggest dream in life was: _____

A lesson he taught me that i still live by: _____

Still With Me

The bed feels wide, the nights fall slow,

Yet in the hush, your echoes grow.

A hand once held, a laugh, a glance

They drift through time like softened dance.

Not every tear becomes a flood,

Some bring calm like morning's mud.

A quiet light, a steady flame,

That whispers gently your sweet name.

Though loss still hums beneath my days,

There are moments you find your ways.

And in those moments, kind and true,

I feel my heart still beats with you.

DEALING WITH THE SHOCK OF LOSS

"Sometimes the most shocking moments teach us who we are."
— Shonda Rhimes

Dear husband, the moment i realized you were truly gone _____

_____

_____

_____

I didn't know what to say. all i could do was _____

_____

_____

_____

I still hear_____

_____

_____

Every time i close my eyes, i _____

_____

_____

I went into autopilot that day because i couldn't _____

_____

_____

_____

DEALING WITH THE SHOCK OF LOSS

"The world is full of suffering. It is also full of overcoming it."
— Helen Keller

My body reacted in ways i didn't expect, like _____

_____

_____

I kept hoping it was a mistake because _____

_____

_____

I still remember where i _____

_____

_____

_____

That day felt like a blur. i remember _____

_____

_____

That day changed me. i no longer _____

_____

_____

_____

ACCEPTING THE TRUTH LITTLE BY LITTLE

"The first step toward change is awareness. The second step is acceptance."
— Nathaniel Branden

My love, sometimes i still think i'll see you walk through the door
and say_____

_____

_____

Some mornings, i wake up and forget_____

_____

_____

I still expect your name to pop up on my phone saying _____

_____

_____

I pretend you're just away for a short time and _____

_____

_____

_____

I sometimes talk out loud like you're still here, especially when

_____

_____

_____

ACCEPTING THE TRUTH LITTLE BY LITTLE

"Facts do not cease to exist because they are ignored."
— Aldous Huxley

I pretend everything is okay when _____

_____

_____

_____

I hold onto your favorite things like you're _____

_____

_____

I still hear your laughter sometimes and think maybe _____

_____

_____

I keep looking for signs that _____

_____

_____

_____

I carry this little denial in my heart because _____

_____

_____

_____

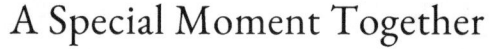

A Special Moment Together

Place for Photo

Place for Photo

Place for Photo

13

A Space for Cherished Memories

SORTING THROUGH CONFUSING THOUGHTS

"It's okay to be confused. Confusion is the route to all clarity."
— Shannon L. Alder

Dear husband, i don't understand why _____

_____

_____

I wish someone could explain _____

_____

_____

_____

I keep trying to make sense of _____

_____

_____

_____

I wonder if i should be _____

_____

_____

I'm not sure how to answer people when _____

_____

_____

_____

SORTING THROUGH CONFUSING THOUGHTS

"When you're lost in those woods, it sometimes
takes you a while to realize that you are lost."
— Patrick Ness

I find myself forgetting _____

_____

_____

Some days, i feel _____

_____

_____

_____

I ask myself over and over if i _____

_____

_____

I keep looking for answers about _____

_____

_____

_____

Dear husband, i just wish i could _____

_____

_____

_____

FACING FEAR AND MOVING FORWARD

"Fear has two meanings: Forget Everything And Run
or Face Everything And Rise. The choice is yours."
— Zig Ziglar

Dear Soulmate, since you've been gone, i'm afraid that_____
_____
_____

Some days, i wake up afraid that _____
_____
_____

I'm afraid of facing the world without _____
_____
_____
_____

I keep thinking about the future and wondering how_____
_____
_____
_____

I don't know what scares me more, missing you or_____
_____
_____
_____

FACING FEAR AND MOVING FORWARD

*"I learned that courage was not
the absence of fear, but the triumph over it."*
— Nelson Mandela

Sometimes i avoid certain places because i'm afraid _____

_____

_____

I wish fear didn't _____

_____

_____

I'm afraid to talk about you sometimes because i _____

_____

_____

My Love, if you were here, i know you'd tell me to _____

_____

_____

One step at a time, just like you taught me, i _____

_____

_____

HANDLING ANGER IN A HEALTHY WAY

*"Holding onto anger is like drinking poison
and expecting the other person to die."*
— Buddha

Dear Husband, i get so mad at myself for_____

_____

_____

_____

I never thought i'd carry this much anger about _____

_____

_____

_____

I didn't realize how precious our_____

_____

_____

I get upset when people say things like_____

_____

_____

_____

I try to stay calm, but when i think about the _____

_____

_____

HANDLING ANGER IN A HEALTHY WAY

"For every minute you remain angry, you give
up sixty seconds of peace of mind."
— Ralph Waldo Emerson

I didn't think i would feel _____

_____

_____

_____

I'm mad that i didn't hold onto _____

_____

_____

_____

When people try to comfort me, sometimes it makes me feel ____

_____

_____ but _____

_____

_____

I just want you to know that even though i'm angry, i still _____

_____

_____

_____

LETTING GO OF REGRET AND "WHAT-IFS"

Guilt is perhaps the most painful companion to death."
— Elisabeth Kübler-Ross

Dear soulmate, i feel guilty that i _____

_____

_____

I regret not doing more when you needed me to _____

_____

_____

_____

I didn't realize how important it was to _____

_____

_____

I still carry guilt about the time i _____

_____

_____

_____

Sometimes i wonder if you knew how much i _____

_____

_____

_____

LETTING GO OF REGRET AND "WHAT-IFS"

"Guilt is always hungry, don't let it consume you."
— Terri Guillemets

If I had just one more day with you, i would _____

_____

_____

_____

I wish i had listened more when you told me that _____

_____

_____

I wish i had been more patient when _____

_____

_____

_____

I blame myself for not noticing sooner that _____

_____

_____

My love, if you could talk to me now, i know you'd tell me _____

_____

_____

_____

FREE YOURSELF FROM SHAME

"The less you talk about your shame, the more power it has."
— Brené Brown

My love, sometimes i feel ashamed _____

_____

_____

_____

I feel embarrassed when people see me_____

_____

_____

I avoid certain people because i'm afraid they'll think _____

_____

_____

Sometimes i catch myself lying about _____

_____

_____

_____

I feel ashamed when i remember our argument about_____

_____

_____

_____

FREE YOURSELF FROM SHAME

"Never feel shame for trying and failing, for he who has never failed is he who has never tried."
— Og Mandino

I've been hiding my true feelings about _____

_____

_____

I avoid sharing my_____

_____

_____

I pretend I'm _____

_____

_____

_____

I know i shouldn't blame myself for_____

_____

_____ but_____

_____

_____

And then i will reach the end of my healing process and feel ____

_____

_____

BREAKING THE SILENCE

"Speak your truth, even if your voice shakes."
— Maggie Kuhn

My love, there were things i wanted to say but didn't know how

_____

_____

_____

I wish we had talked more openly about _____

_____

_____

I still wonder if you knew how much it hurt me when _____

_____

_____

I regret not being more honest with you about _____

_____

_____

I hope you know that even in our hardest moments, i _____

_____

_____

_____

BREAKING THE SILENCE

"There is no greater agony than bearing an untold story inside you."
— Maya Angelou

I'll never know why you couldn't say_____

_____

_____

_____

I hope you understood why i reacted the way i did when _____

_____

_____

_____

I still question why you _____

_____

_____

Even though we had disagreements, i never stopped _____

_____

_____

_____

I forgive you for all_____

_____

_____

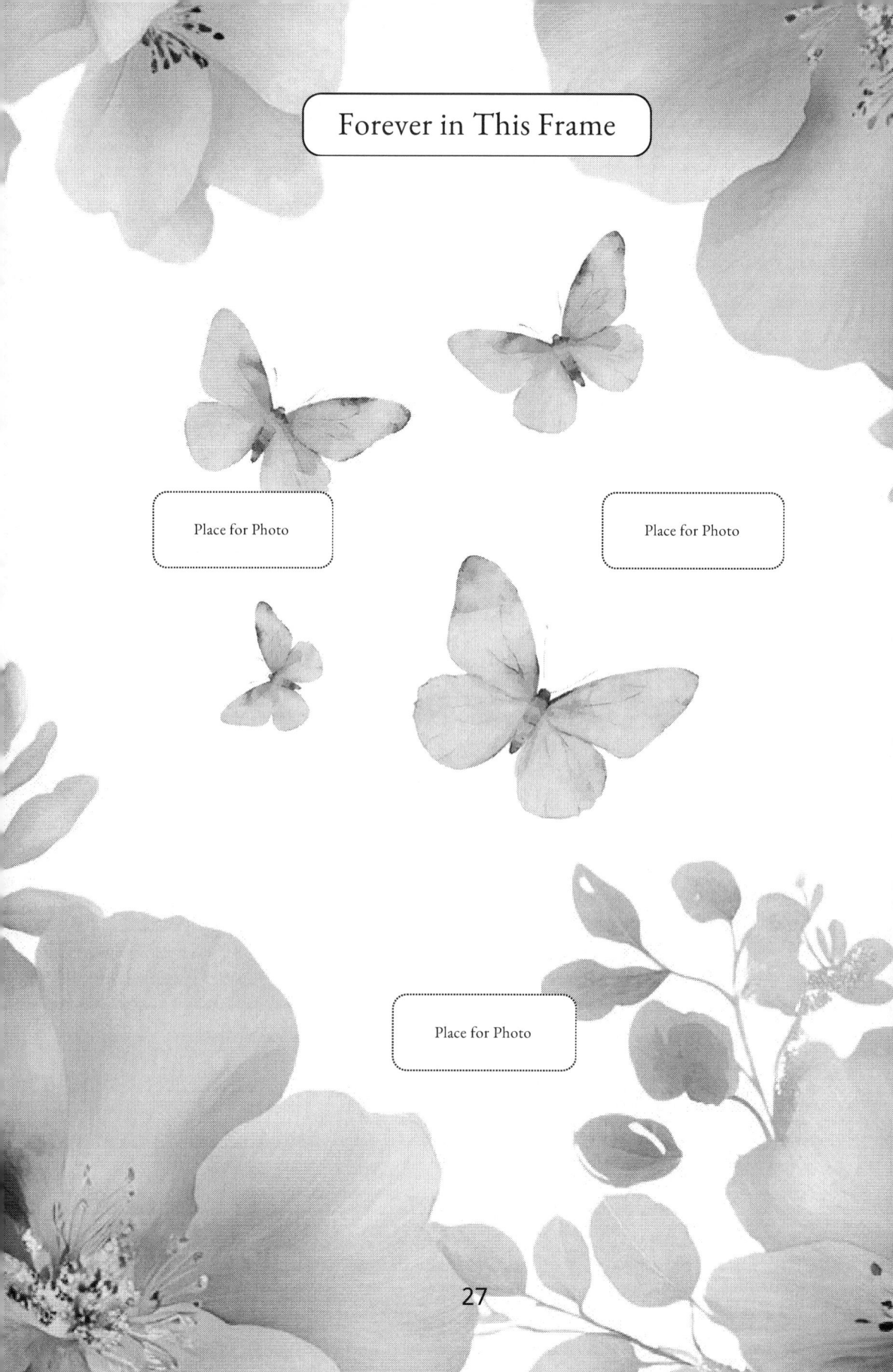

Forever in This Frame

Place for Photo

Place for Photo

Place for Photo

A Collection of Wise Lessons

COPING WITH FEELING ALONE

"The greatest thing in the world is to know how to belong to oneself."
— Michel de Montaigne

My love, since you've been gone, i feel so alone_____

_____

_____

I miss having you here when _____

_____

_____

_____

Sometimes i sit in the quiet and pretend you're still _____

_____

_____

_____

Since you left, i don't know who to turn to when i need_____

_____

_____

There are times when i want to talk to you so badly, but instead,

i just_____

_____

_____

COPING WITH FEELING ALONE

"Loneliness and the feeling of being unwanted is the most terrible poverty."
— Mother Teresa

I miss our conversations about:

- ◆ _____
- ◆ _____
- ◆ _____
- ◆ _____
- ◆ _____
- ◆ _____
- ◆ _____

I miss your advice, especially:

- ◆ _____
- ◆ _____
- ◆ _____
- ◆ _____
- ◆ _____
- ◆ _____

My love, even in my loneliness, i still carry your presence in _____

_____

_____

MANAGING DEEP SADNESS

"Every human walks around with a certain kind of sadness. They may not wear it on their sleeves, but it's there if you look deep."
— Taraji P. Henson

I find myself crying when i think about _____

_____

_____

_____

I wish i could call you right now and tell you _____

_____

_____

The hardest part of this sadness is _____

_____

_____

I try to stay strong, but sometimes deep down i'm_____

_____

_____

_____

I never knew missing someone could feel like _____

_____

_____

_____

MANAGING DEEP SADNESS

"Sometimes we need to sit with our sadness, let it wash over us, and trust that it won't last forever."
— Unknown

It hurts to think about the things you'll never get to see, like:

- ◆ _____
- ◆ _____
- ◆ _____
- ◆ _____
- ◆ _____
- ◆ _____
- ◆ _____
- ◆ _____
- ◆ _____
- ◆ _____

My love, even in my sadness, i hold onto _____

_____

_____

I know you wouldn't want me to be this sad _____

_____

_____

_____

HOLDING THE MEMORIES

The desire to reach for the stars is ambitious. The desire to reach hearts is wise."
— Maya Angelou

My love, i miss the way you always knew what i needed, especially

when _____

_____

I still remember the quiet mornings we shared, drinking _____

_____ and talking about _____

_____

You always knew how to make me smile, whether it was bringing

home _____

_____ or _____

_____ or _____

I think about the times we built things together, whether it was

_____

and _____you always had a plan.

I miss the way we used to drive around listening to _____

_____

_____ and singing along to _____

_____ and laughing about _____

_____

HOLDING THE MEMORIES

"Sometimes, only one person is missing, and the whole world seems depopulated."
— Alphonse de Lamartine

You always made sure i felt special, even _____

_____

_____

I miss the way we used to cook together, how you'd prepare _____

_____

_____ while i made _____

_____

I still think about how you took the time to teach me how to fix

_____

_____ making me feel capable and strong.

I still remember how you took me shopping and let me pick out

_____ and _____

_____ and _____

_____

I loved how we used to go on trips to _____

_____ and _____

_____ and _____

_____ always making the best memories outdoors.

34

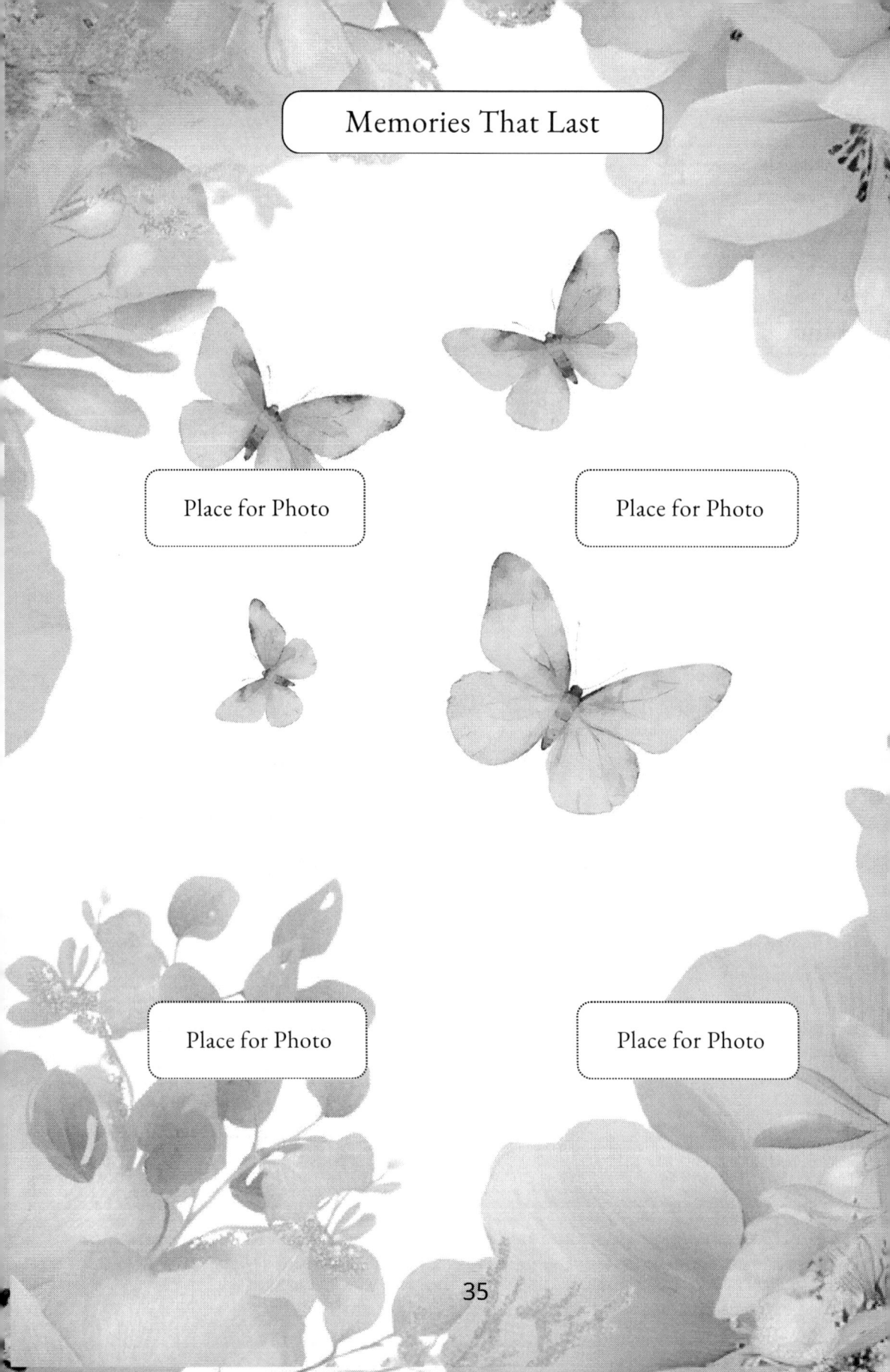

Memories That Last

Place for Photo

Place for Photo

Place for Photo

Place for Photo

Moments and Things That Keep Husband's Memory Alive

_____

_____

_____

_____

_____

_____

_____

_____

_____

_____

_____

_____

_____

_____

_____

_____

_____

_____

FINDING SMALL MOMENTS OF PEACE

"The moment of relief is when you realize you don't have to carry it all alone."
— Unknown

Dear Soulmate, i know you're no longer in pain, and that brings me

some peace because _____

_____

_____

Even in my hardest moments, it helps to know you're _____

_____

_____

Letting go of the pain doesn't mean letting go of you, and i'm

learning that _____

_____

_____

Knowing you're at peace makes it a little easier to _____

_____

_____

Even when i cry, i also feel relief _____

_____

_____

_____

FINDING SMALL MOMENTS OF PEACE

"Breathe. Let go. And remind yourself that this very moment is the only
one you know you have for sure."
— Oprah Winfrey

I can finally sleep a little better knowing that _____

_____

_____

_____

Sometimes, i close my eyes and feel you near, and that brings me

_____

_____

I used to be so afraid of losing you, but now i realize _____

_____

_____

I take a deep breath and feel a strange sense of relief when

i remember that you're _____

_____

_____

I know you wouldn't want me to live in sadness_____

_____

_____

_____

MAKING ROOM FOR ACCEPTANCE

"Happiness can exist only in acceptance."
— George Orwell

Dear Husband, i will always love you, but i am learning to live with

_____

_____

It's taken me time, but i finally understand that _____

_____

_____

_____

I have learned to be grateful for_____

_____

_____

_____ instead of only focusing on what i've lost.

Even though i'll always miss you, i am _____

_____

_____

I used to think i couldn't go on without you, but now i know

_____

_____

_____

MAKING ROOM FOR ACCEPTANCE

"Understanding is the first step to acceptance, and only with
acceptance can there be recovery."
— J.K. Rowling

My Love, i am beginning to see that you will always be with me

when _____

_____

I'm slowly learning to let go of what i can't change and _____

_____

_____

_____

I'm starting to understand that love and loss can exist _____

_____

_____

_____

I'm accepting that healing happens in small steps, like _____

_____

_____

_____

I trust that my heart can hold both grief and _____

_____

_____

HONORING THE PAST WITH GRATITUDE

"Gratitude is not only the greatest of virtues, but the parent of all others."
— Marcus Tullius Cicero

Even though you're gone, i am thankful that i can still _____

_____

_____

I am grateful for the strength you gave me, especially when i

_____

_____

Your kindness and wisdom still guide me when _____

_____

_____

I will always be thankful for the lessons you taught me, like:

- ◆ _____

- ◆ _____

- ◆ _____

- ◆ _____

- ◆ _____

- ◆ _____

- ◆ _____

- ◆ _____

HONORING THE PAST WITH GRATITUDE

"The more grateful I am, the more beauty I see."
— Mary Davis

I feel gratitude when i think about how much you _____

_____

_____

I appreciate the way you shaped my life by _____

_____

_____

Every time i think of you, i remember to be thankful for _____

_____

_____

_____

I want to thank you for_____

- ◆ _____

- ◆ _____

- ◆ _____

- ◆ _____

- ◆ _____

- ◆ _____

- ◆ _____

KEEPING YOUR HUSBAND'S LOVE IN YOUR HEART

"The love we give away is the only love we keep."
— Elbert Hubbard

Dear Husband, i will always love you _____

_____

_____

One of the greatest gifts of your love was _____

_____

_____

I still feel your love when _____

_____

_____

_____

I see the love you gave me reflected in _____

_____

_____

_____

I carry your love with me every day, especially when _____

_____

_____

_____

KEEPING YOUR HUSBAND'S LOVE IN YOUR HEART

"Where there is love there is life."
— Mahatma Gandhi

I hope i make you proud _____

_____

_____

Your love taught me how to _____

_____

_____

Your love still guides me when i have to _____

_____

_____

_____

I think of you every time i hear_____

_____

_____

_____ because it reminds me of your love.

If i could hug you one more time, i'd say_____

_____

_____

_____

A Photo of Love and Laughter

Place for Photo

Place for Photo

Place for Photo

Place for Photo

Place for Photo

Place for Photo

A Frame for Meaningful Advice

FINDING HOPE EVEN ON HARD DAYS

"Even the darkest night will end and the sun will rise."
— Victor Hugo

I find hope in knowing that one day, i will _____

_____

_____

_____

I am starting to see signs that things will get better, like _____

◆ _____

◆ _____

◆ _____

◆ _____

◆ _____

There was a time when i thought i'd never feel okay again, but now

_____

_____

_____

Even on my hardest days, i remind myself that _____

_____

_____

_____

FINDING HOPE EVEN ON HARD DAYS

"When you're at the end of your rope, tie a knot and hold on."
— Theodore Roosevelt

I know you'd tell me to keep dreaming, so i will _____

_____

_____

_____

I'm starting to believe that joy can exist alongside _____

_____

_____

_____

Dear Soulmate, i will carry your lessons with me as i step into

_____

_____

_____

I am looking forward to_____

_____

_____

_____

_____ because i know you'd want me to find joy again.

HEALING AND STRENGTH

"The only way that we can live is if we grow. The only way that we can grow
is if we change."
— C. JoyBell C.

Through this journey, i have learned to appreciate _____

_____

_____

_____

I have learned about my own strength because _____

_____

_____

_____

I never imagined i could heal in this way, but i am starting to

_____

_____

I have become more patient with myself and _____

_____

_____

My Love, i never thought i'd be able to _____

_____

_____

_____ but now i realize i can.

HEALING AND STRENGTH

"Be not afraid of growing slowly, be afraid only of standing still."
— Chinese Proverb

I have discovered a new perspective on life since _____

_____

_____

_____

I have realized that growth comes from: _____

- ◆ _____

- ◆ _____

- ◆ _____

- ◆ _____

- ◆ _____

- ◆ _____

- ◆ _____

- ◆ _____

If you were here, i know you'd remind me that strength is _____

_____

_____

_____

_____

SELF-CARE WHILE YOU HEAL

"Act as if what you do makes a difference. It does."
— William James

To improve my daily life, i plan to focus on my sleep, meals, and

exercise, so i can _____

_____

_____

I plan to set a consistent sleep schedule by going to bed at _____

_____ and waking up at _____

To improve my sleep, i'll avoid _____

_____

_____ before bed and instead focus on _____

_____

_____

My plan for improving my appetite is to start each day with

a healthy breakfast like _____

_____

_____

To boost my appetite, i'll try eating smaller portions of_____

_____

_____throughout the day.

SELF-CARE WHILE YOU HEAL

"The journey of a thousand miles begins with one step."
— Lao Tzu

My goal for a balanced appetite is to include _____

_____

_____

_____ in my meals.

I plan to schedule time for sports activities like _____

_____

_____ at least _____ times a week.

To make exercise enjoyable, i'll combine sports with fun activities

like _____

_____

To improve my physical and mental health, i'll incorporate sports

such as _____

_____

_____ into my weekly routine.

I plan to use sports as a way to manage stress by _____

_____

_____

_____ whenever i feel overwhelmed.

YOU ARE NOT ALONE ON THIS JOURNEY

(A GENTLE MESSAGE FOR BEREAVED PEOPLE)

"One kind word can warm three winter months."
— Japanese Proverb

You are not alone in this. we will find our way through this

grief, together and _____

_____

You don't have to be strong every moment. some days, just

breathing is enough and _____

_____

_____

When the world feels like it has moved on, i want you to know

_____

_____

It's okay if you still expect to hear your husband's voice or see

them walk through the door, this _____

_____

You don't have to feel okay all the time, but when peace finds

you, even for a moment, let yourself _____

_____

_____

YOU ARE NOT ALONE ON THIS JOURNEY

(A GENTLE MESSAGE FOR BEREAVED PEOPLE)

"The best way to find yourself is to lose yourself in the service of others."
— Mahatma Gandhi

Some days, acceptance will feel impossible, and other days, it will feel like a quiet understanding. both are part of healing, just _____

_____

_____

You might feel lost right now, but i promise you, one day, you will find _____

_____

Every memory, every lesson, every moment you shared is a gift that will always be yours. let gratitude be your _____

_____

_____

Even in solitude, you are connected to those who love you _____

_____

_____

Drink water, get fresh air, and find small ways to take care _____

_____

_____

A Memory Captured for Me

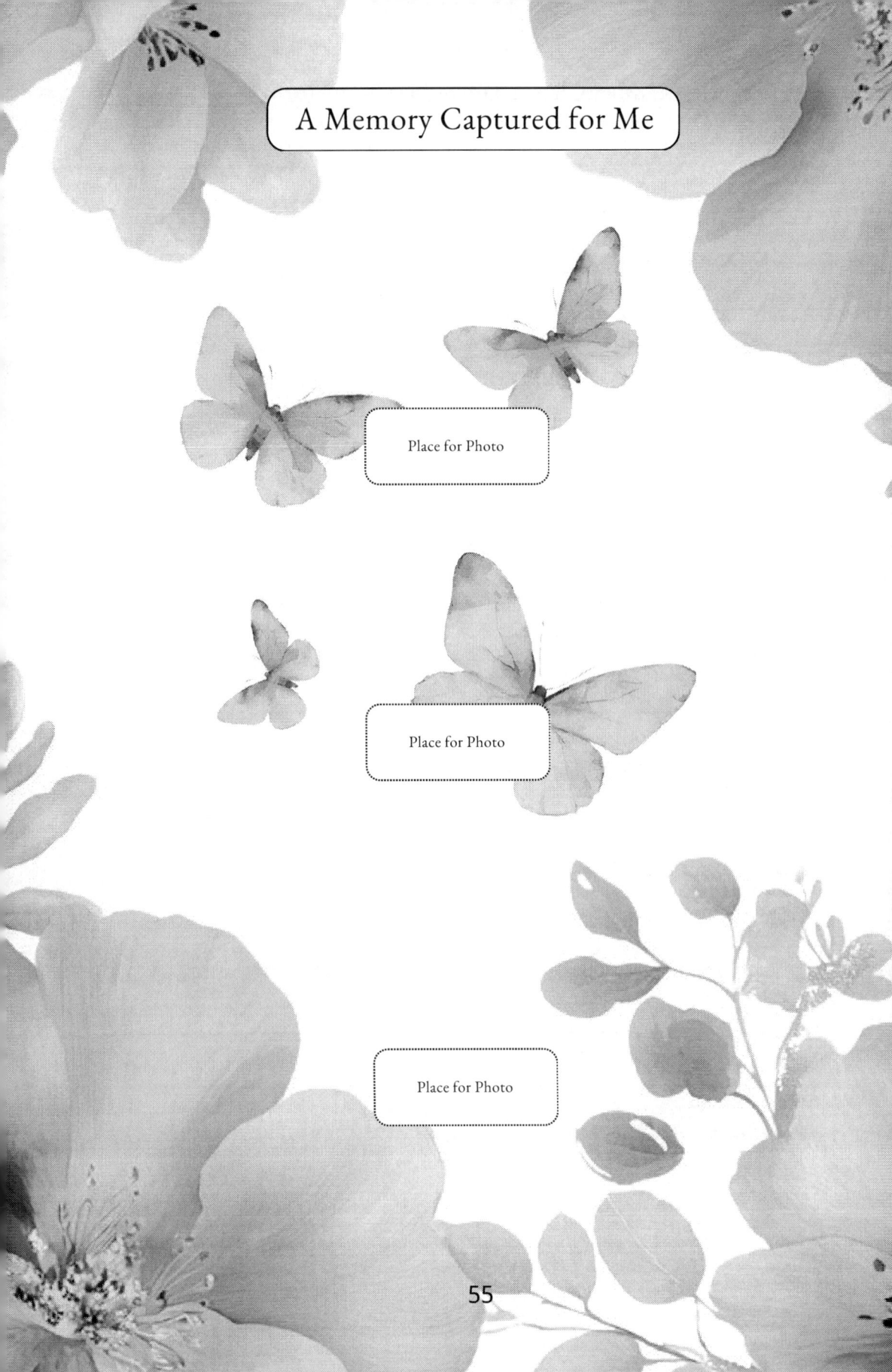

Place for Photo

Place for Photo

Place for Photo

This Is My Healing Story

_____

_____

_____

_____

_____

_____

_____

_____

_____

_____

_____

_____

_____

_____

_____

_____

_____

_____

_____

_____

_____

Hope Like the Morning Light

Hope is quiet, soft, and small,

A flicker where the shadows fall.

It whispers through the breaking dawn,

A promise that the night moves on.

I thought i'd never breathe the same,

That joy would never call my name.

But hope still hums beneath the pain,

A gentle pull, a soft refrain.

It doesn't rush, it doesn't shout,

Yet somehow, light still finds a route.

Through every tear, through loss and ache,

Hope reminds, my heart won't break.

THE END

By Evelyn Harrington

Thank you for allowing this journal to be a part of your journey. If you've filled these pages, even a little, know that you have already taken steps toward healing. If you found yourself pausing, struggling, or needing to step away, that's okay too. healing is not about speed, it's about giving yourself grace in the moments you need it most.

I wrote this journal with the hope that it would offer you comfort, reflection, and a safe space to express what's inside. no words will ever replace the presence of the one you lost, but I hope you have found a way to hold their love close, through your thoughts, your memories, and your own path forward.

I Am Grateful to You

If this journal has helped you in any way, i would be truly grateful for your support. Leaving a review, sharing your experience, or recommending this journal to someone in need allows more people to find comfort and healing through these pages. your words have the power to help others, just as your journey has value in ways you may not yet realize.

With warmth and understanding,
Evelyn Harrington

Made in the USA
Coppell, TX
25 April 2026

76589589R00035